Learning About Zero

Zero means **there are none**.

Trace and write the number. Start at the red dot (●).

How many puppies are there in each group?
Write the numbers.

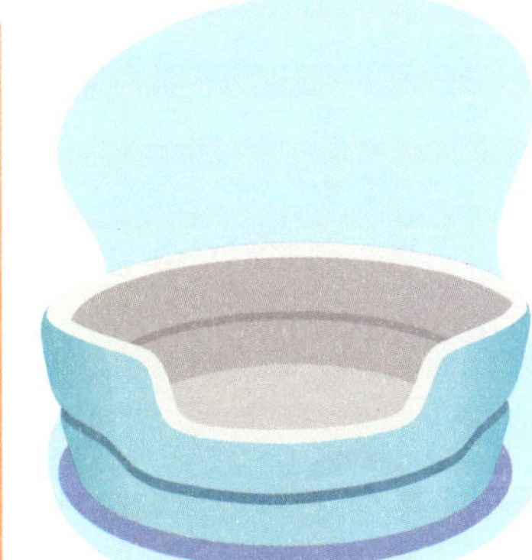

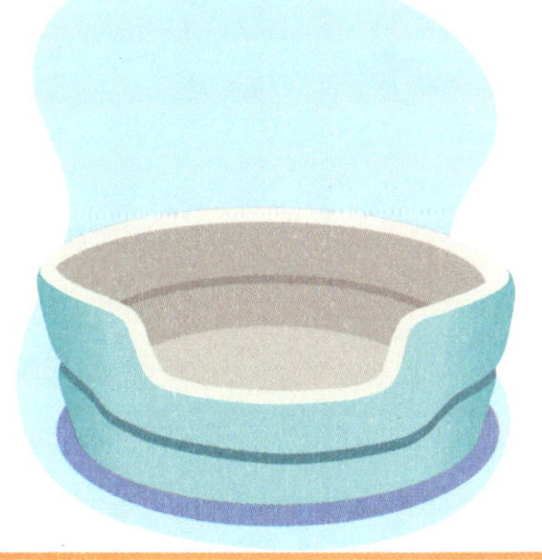

Counting to One and Two

Trace and write the numbers. Start at the red dot (●).

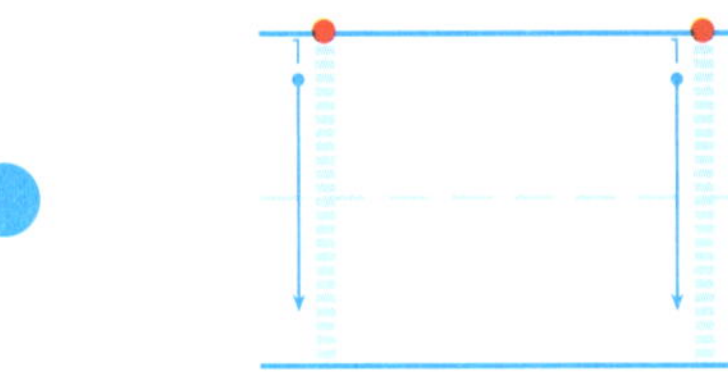

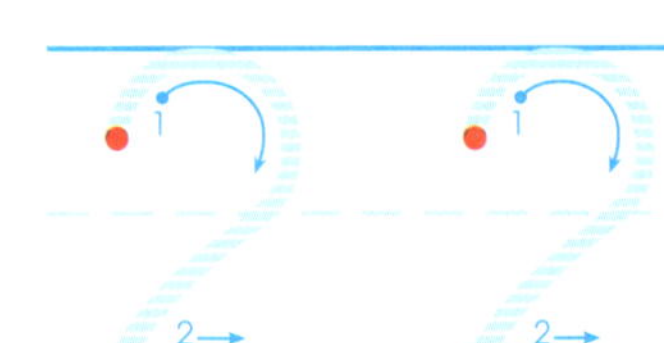

Try This!

Sensory Number Practice
Fill a pie tin with enough salt to cover the bottom completely. Have kids trace numbers in the salt.

How many animals are there in each group? Write the numbers.

Counting to Three and Four

Trace and write the numbers. Start at the red dot (●).

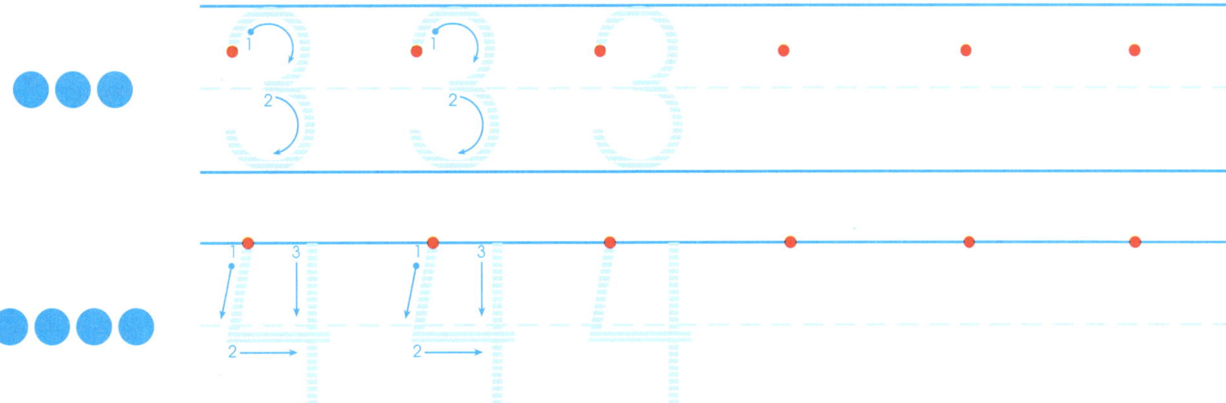

How many animals are there in each group?
Write the numbers.

Inside, Outside, Over

Write the answers.

How many  are **inside** the room? ______________

How many  are **outside** the room? ______________

How many  are **over** the door? ______________

Counting to Five and Six

Trace and write the numbers. Start at the red dot (●).

Giggles

What fish only swims at night?

A starfish!

How many animals are there in each group? Write the numbers.

Counting Shapes

Count the shapes.
Draw **1 more** shape.
Write how many shapes you have now.
The first one is done for you.

Count	Draw	Write

Counting Groups

Draw a line from each number to the correct group.
Write each number by the correct group.
The first one is done for you.

Giggles

What did the momma cow say to the calf?

It's pasture bedtime!

Counting to Seven and Eight

Trace and write the numbers. Start at the red dot (●).

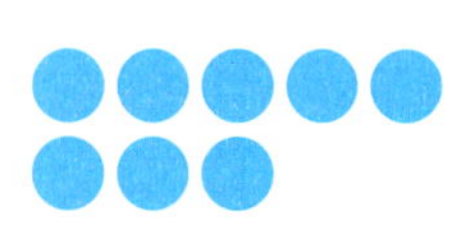

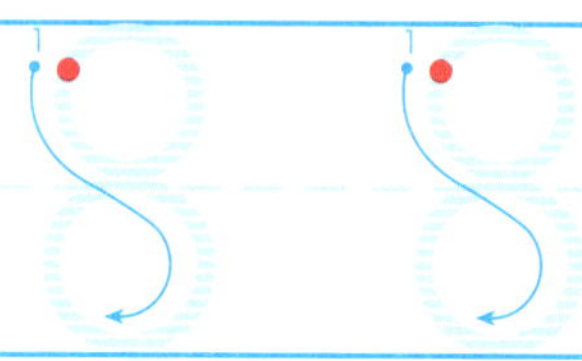

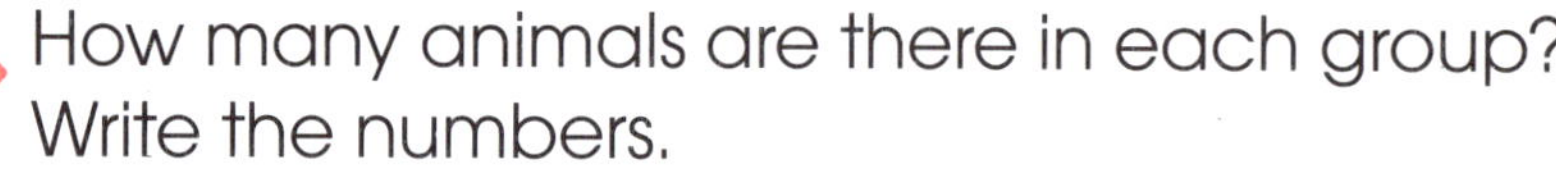

How many animals are there in each group? Write the numbers.

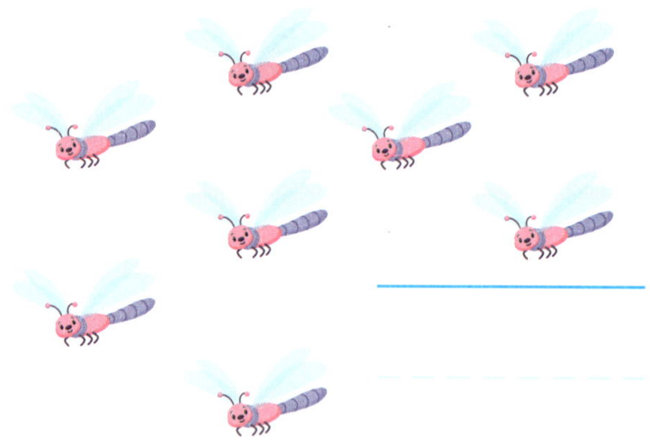

Counting to Nine and Ten

Trace and write the numbers. Start at the red dot (●).

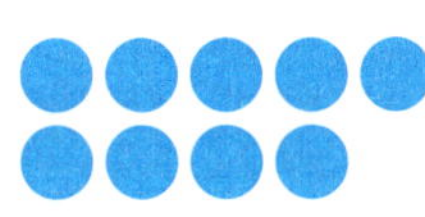

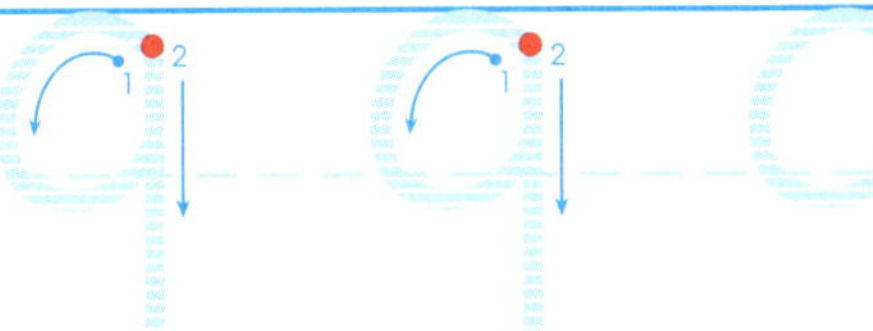

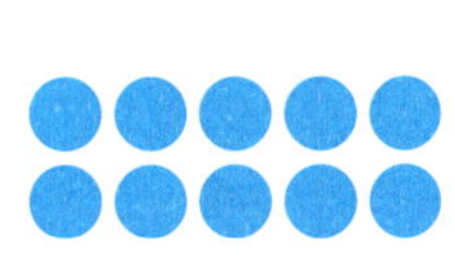

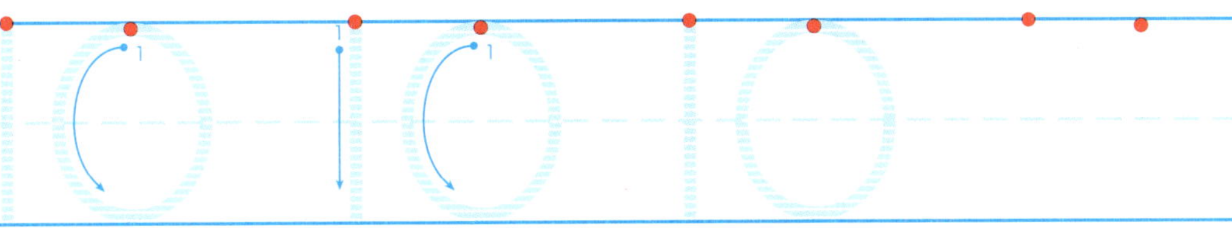

How many animals are there in each group?
Write the numbers.

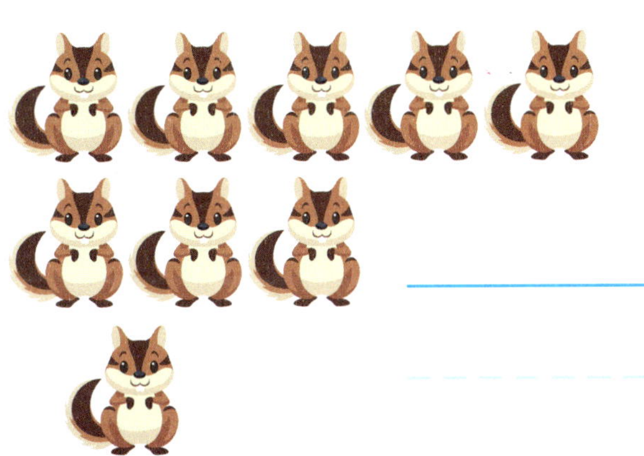

Count and Color

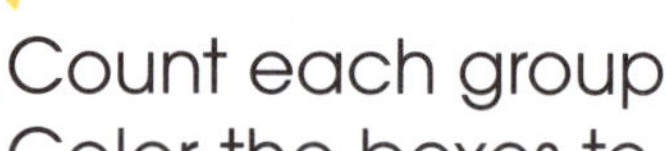

Count each group.
Color the boxes to match the number.
Write the number. The first one is done for you.

Count	Color	Write
		7

Counting to Eleven and Twelve

Trace and write the numbers. Start at the red dot (●).

How many fish are there in each group?
Write the numbers.

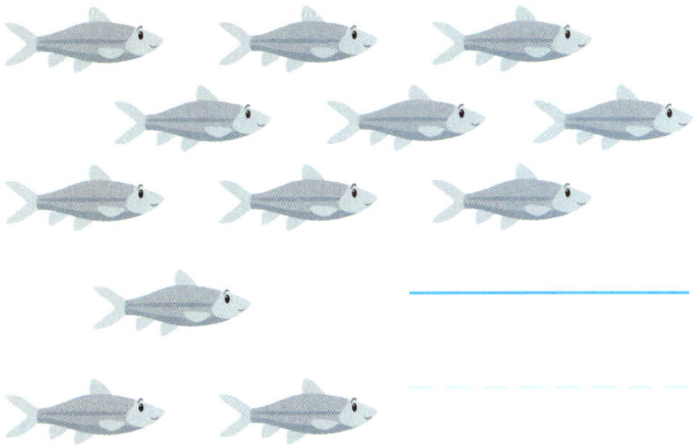

Counting to Thirteen and Fourteen

Trace and write the numbers. Start at the red dot (●).

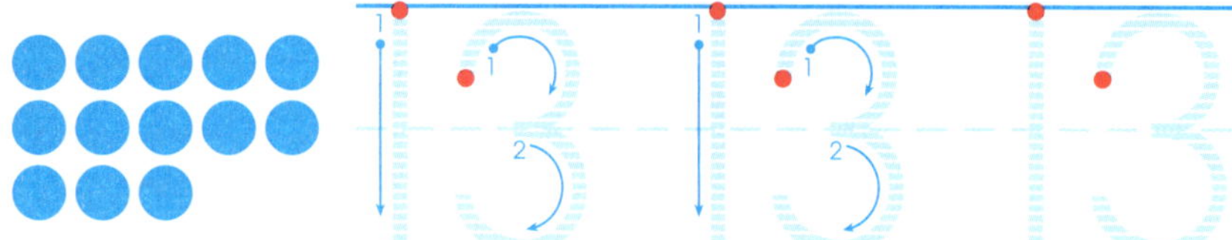

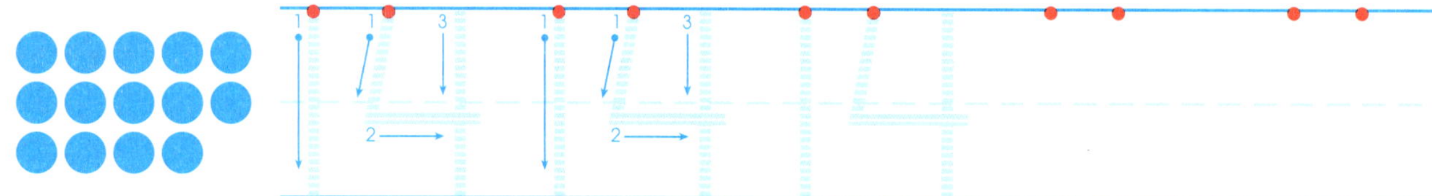

How many balloons are there in each group?
Write the numbers.

Counting to Fifteen and Sixteen

Trace and write the numbers. Start at the red dot (●).

How many marbles are there in each group?
Write the numbers.

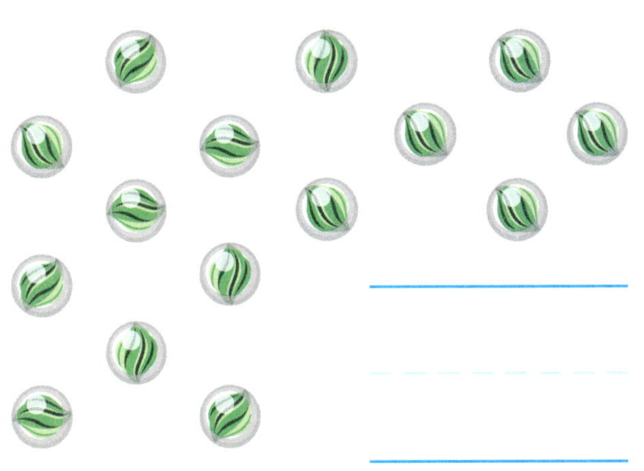

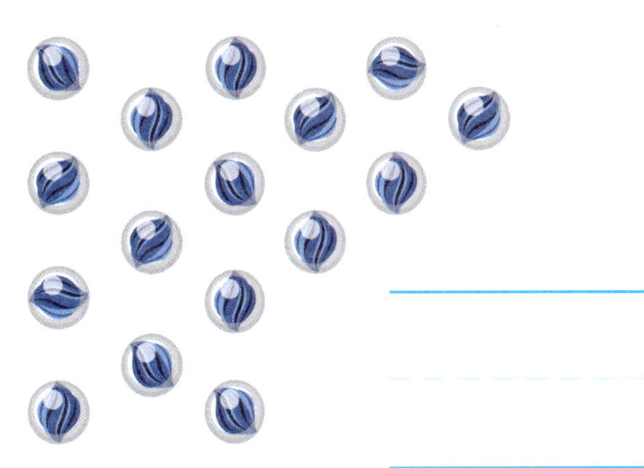

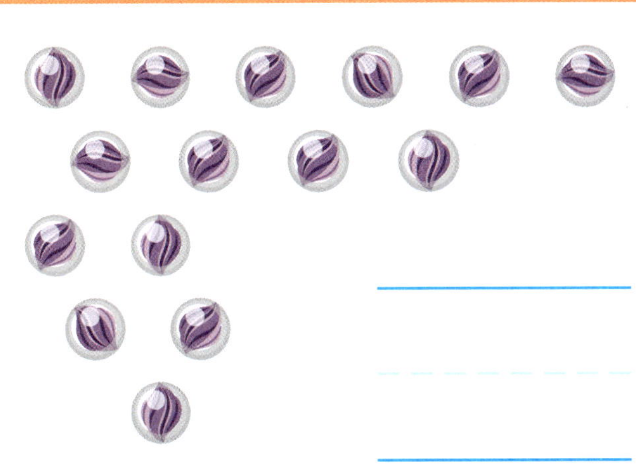

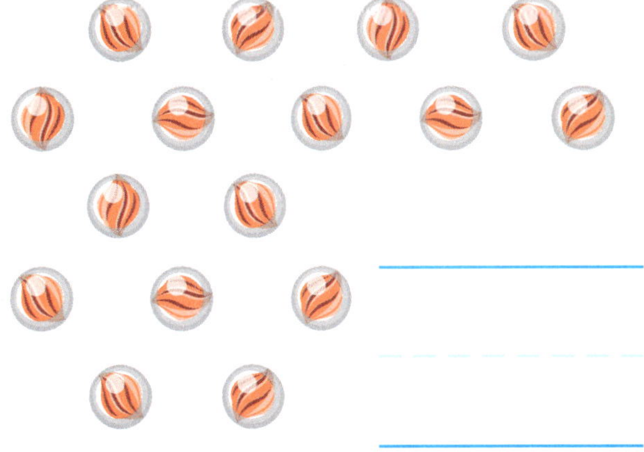

Counting to Seventeen and Eighteen

Trace and write the numbers. Start at the red dot (●).

Giggles
What did the duck say after she bought lip balm?
Put it on my bill! (printed upside down)

How many animals are there in each group? Write the numbers.

Counting to Nineteen and Twenty

Trace and write the numbers. Start at the red dot (●).

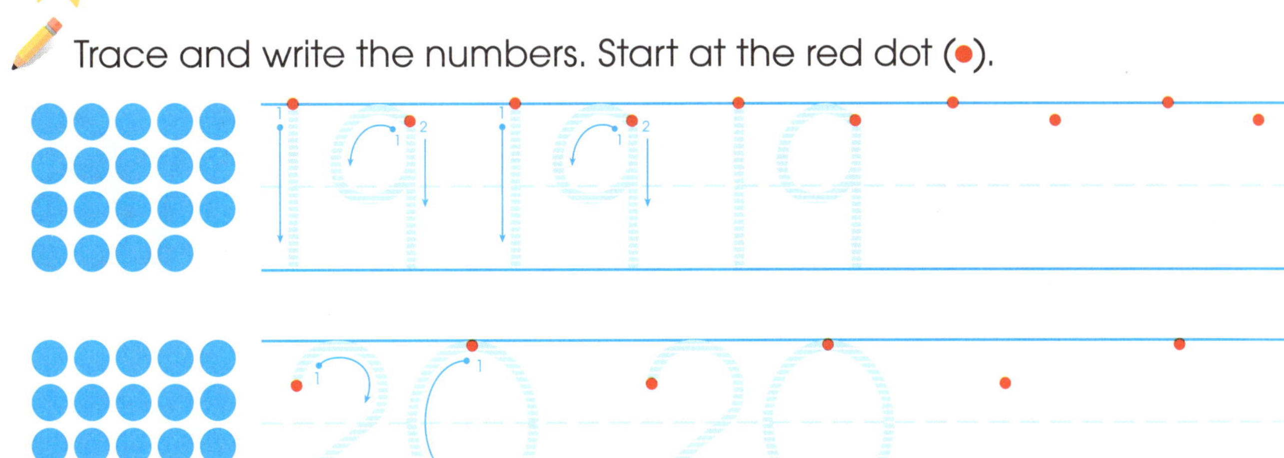

How many things are there in each group?
Write the numbers.

What Number Comes After?

The number **14** comes **after** the number **13**.

12 13 

Write the number that comes **after**.

8 9 ___

5 6 ___

11 12 ___

13 14 ___

17 18 ___

6 7 ___

16 17 ___

10 11 ___

Count to Twenty

Count to **20**.

Write the missing numbers.

Circle the numbers **10** and **20**.

1			4		6	7		9	
	12	13		15			18		20

Color the picture.

20

The Letter A

Trace and write the letters.
Start at the red dot (●).

Color the picture.

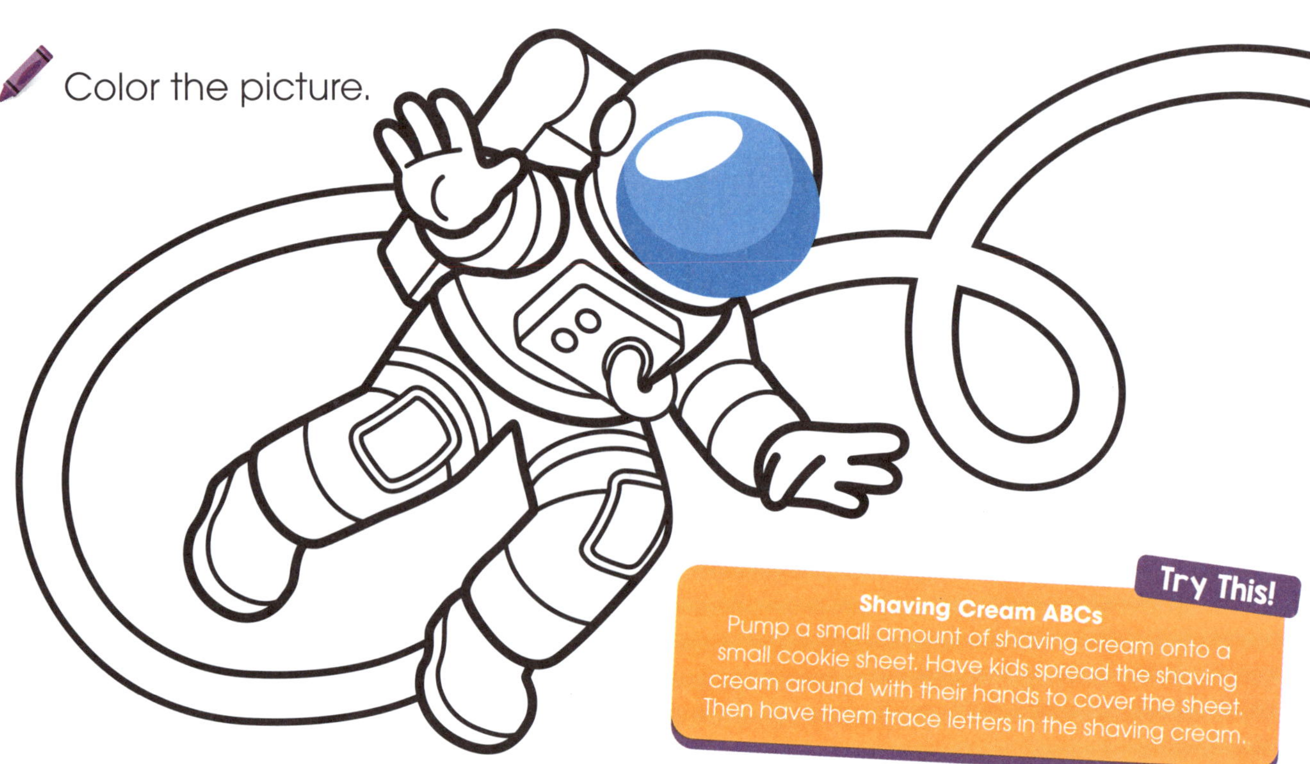

Try This!

Shaving Cream ABCs
Pump a small amount of shaving cream onto a small cookie sheet. Have kids spread the shaving cream around with their hands to cover the sheet. Then have them trace letters in the shaving cream.

Trace the letters to finish the sentence. Start at the red dots (●).

A is for astronaut.

The Letter B

Trace and write the letters.
Start at the red dot (●).

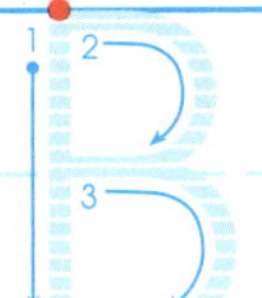

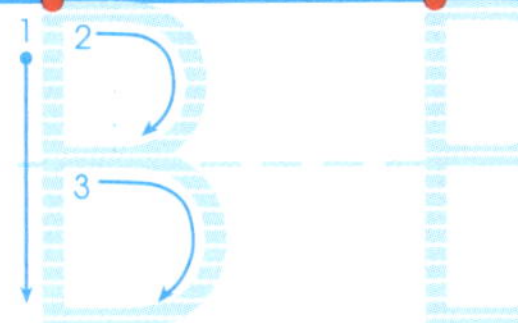

Color the picture.

Trace the letters to finish the sentence. Start at the red dots (●).

B is for bee.

The Letter C

Trace and write the letters.
Start at the red dot (●).

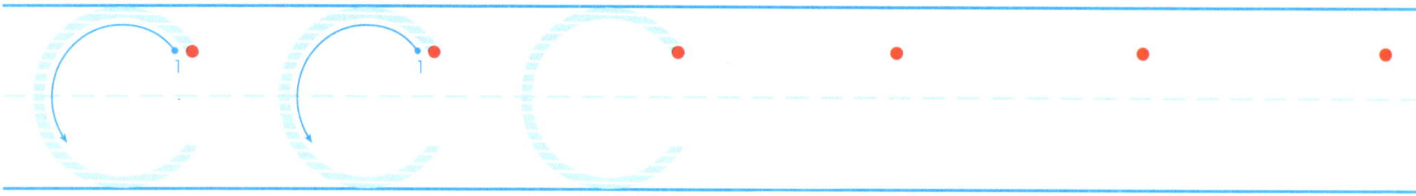

Color the picture.

Trace the letters to finish the sentence. Start at the red dots (●).

C is for cat.

The Letter D

Trace and write the letters.
Start at the red dot (●).

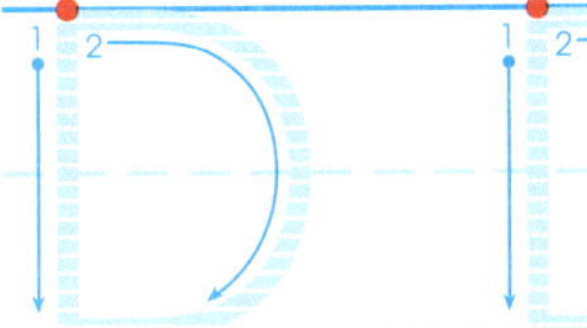

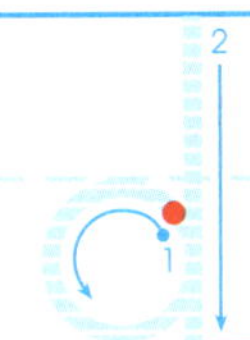

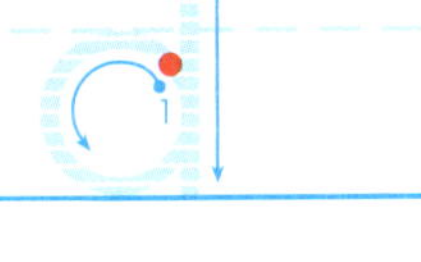

Color the picture.

Trace the letters to finish the sentence. Start at the red dots (●).

D is for dog.

The Letter E

Trace and write the letters.
Start at the red dot (●).

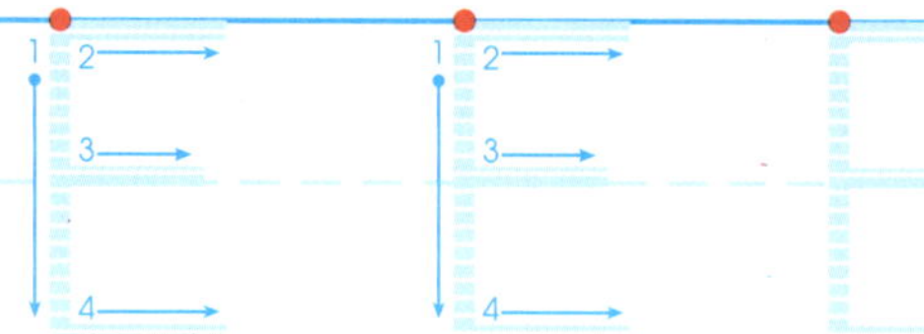

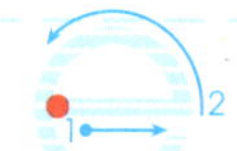

Color the picture.

Trace the letters to finish the sentence. Start at the red dots (●).

E is for elk.

The Letter F

Trace and write the letters.
Start at the red dot (●).

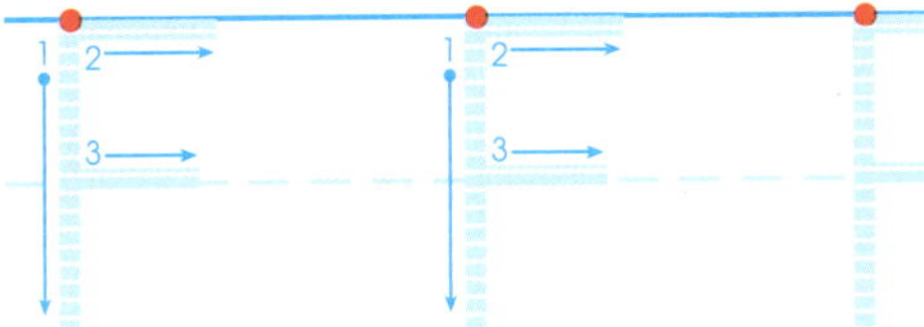

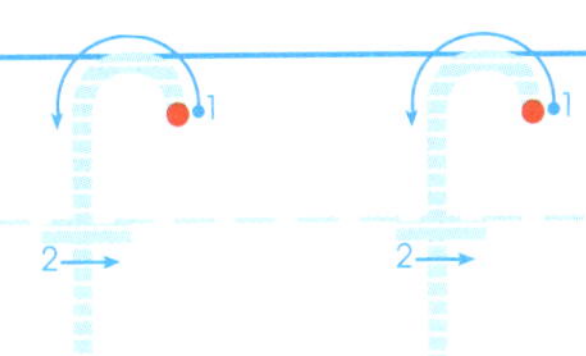

Color the picture.

Giggles

Why are frogs so happy?

They eat whatever bugs them!

Trace the letters to finish the sentence. Start at the red dots (●).

F is for frog.

The Letter G

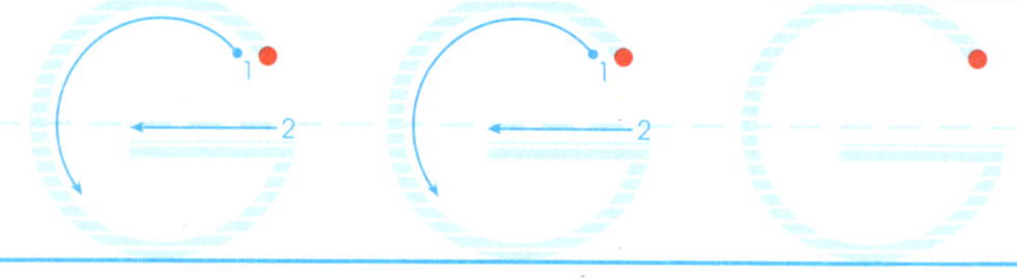

Trace and write the letters.
Start at the red dot (●).

Color the picture.

Trace the letters to finish the sentence. Start at the red dots (●).

G is for goat.

Lots of Letters

Say the name of each picture.
Underline the letters in each row that **begin** the name of the picture.
The first one is done for you.

E f F L f

a d A V a

C o a C c

R b P B b

b d D a D

Matching Letters

Draw a line from each uppercase letter to the matching lowercase letter.

A	c
B	d
C	a
D	b
E	f
F	g
G	e

The Letter H

Trace and write the letters.
Start at the red dot (●).

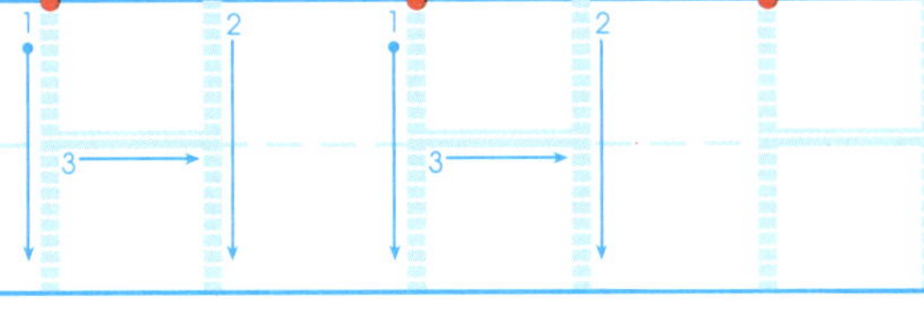

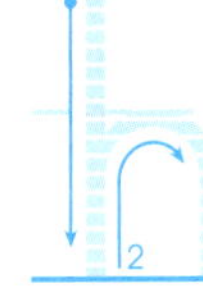

Color the picture.

Trace the letters to finish the sentence. Start at the red dots (●).

H is for hamster.

The Letter I

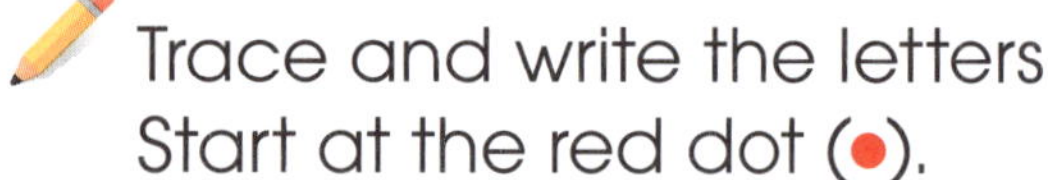

Trace and write the letters.
Start at the red dot (●).

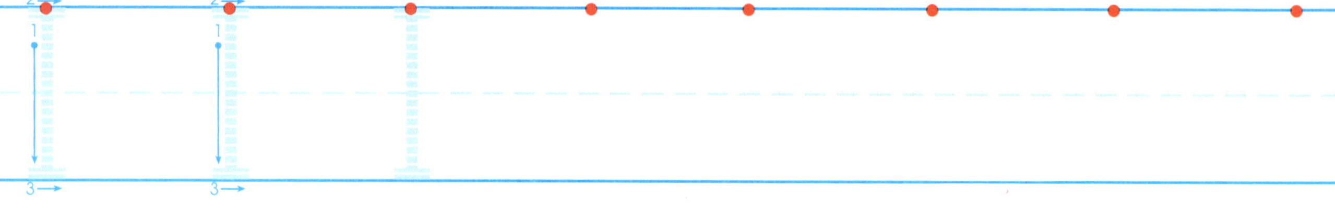

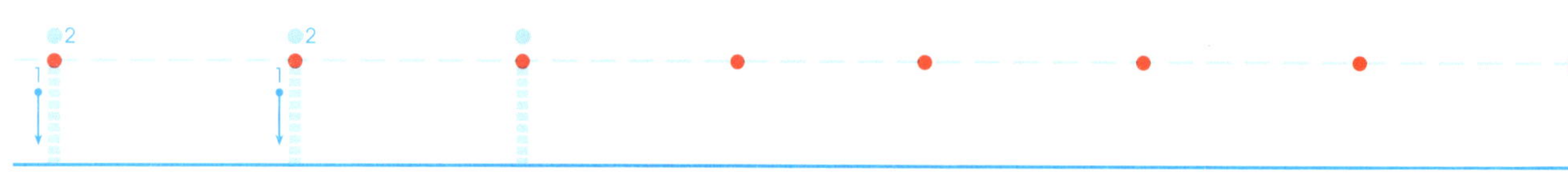

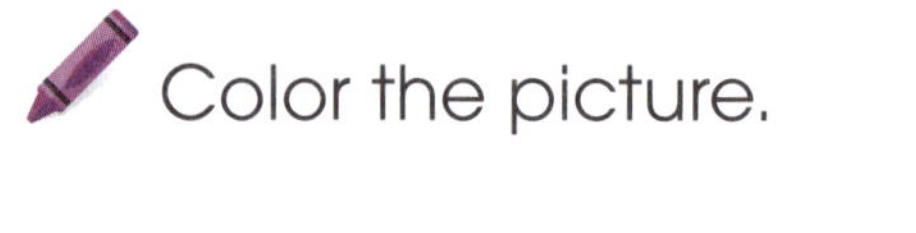

Color the picture.

Fun Fact

Did you know that iguanas have a "third eye" on top of their heads? It looks like a small, pale spot and helps them see light and movement, so they can spot danger from above!

Trace the letters to finish the sentence. Start at the red dots (●).

I is for iguana.

The Letter J

Trace and write the letters.
Start at the red dot (●).

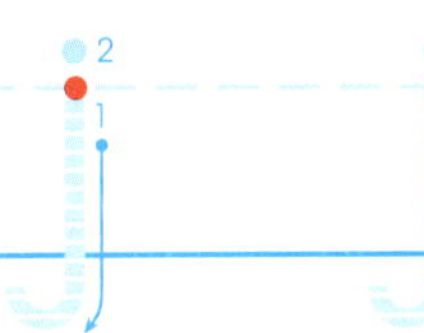

Color the picture.

Trace the letters to finish the sentence. Start at the red dots (●).

J is for jet.

The Letter K

Trace and write the letters.
Start at the red dot (●).

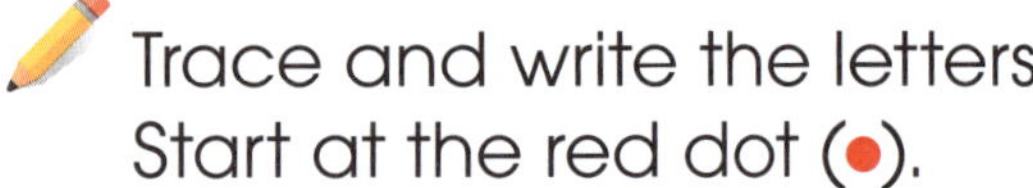

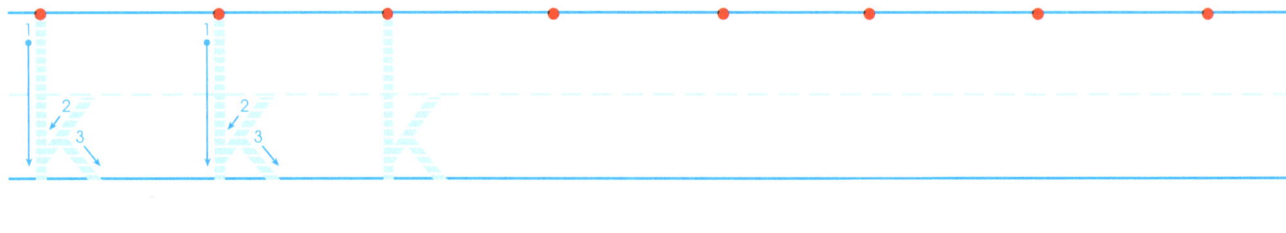

Color the picture.

Trace the letters to finish the sentence. Start at the red dots (●).

K is for kite.

The Letter L

Trace and write the letters.
Start at the red dot (●).

Fun Fact
Lions are the only cats that roar together.

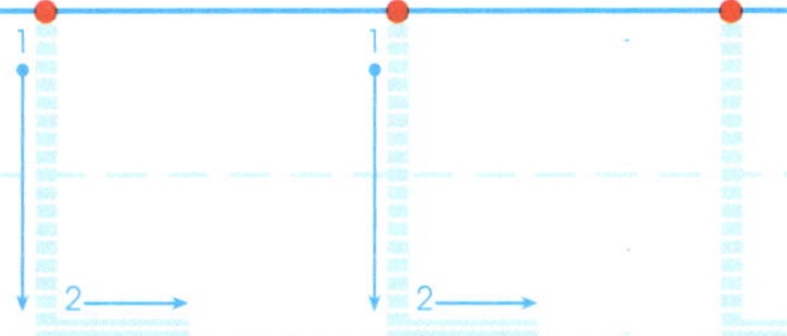

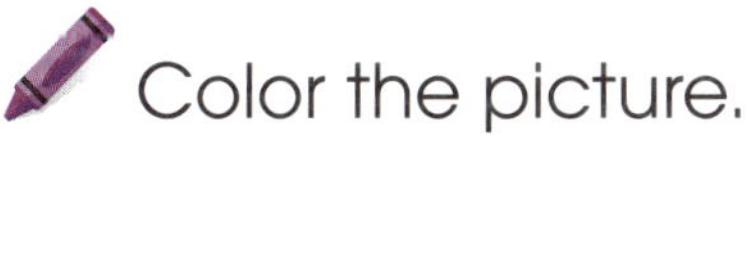

Color the picture.

Trace the letters to finish the sentence. Start at the red dots (●).

L is for lion.

The Letter M

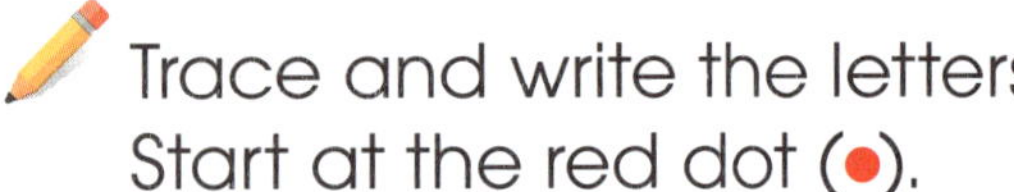

Trace and write the letters.
Start at the red dot (●).

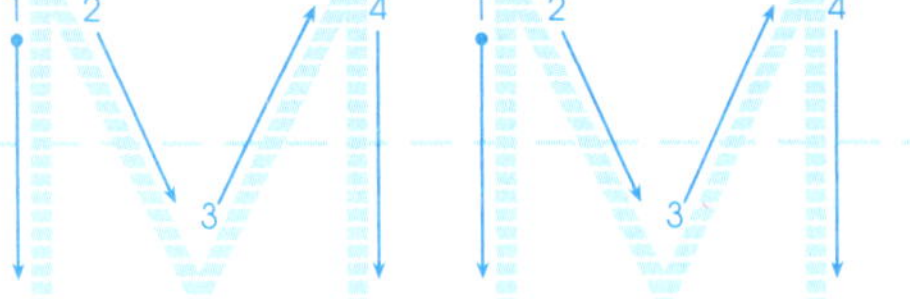

M M M

m m m

Color the picture.

Trace the letters to finish the sentence. Start at the red dots (●).

M is for monkey.

The Letter N

Trace and write the letters.
Start at the red dot (●).

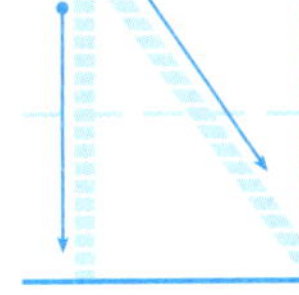

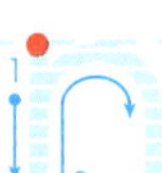

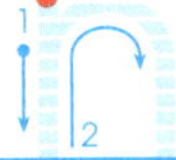

Color the picture.

Trace the letters to finish the sentence. Start at the red dots (●).

 is for 

N is for nest.

Lots of Letters

Say the name of each picture.
Underline the letters in each row that **begin** the name of the picture.

G g b G C

h b H E h

U j J g J

I i T i L

L i l I D

Matching Letters

Draw a line from each uppercase letter to the matching lowercase letter.

H	i
I	j
J	h
K	k
L	m
M	n
N	l

The Letter O

Trace and write the letters.
Start at the red dot (●).

Color the picture.

Trace the letters to finish the sentence. Start at the red dots (●).

is for tter.

The Letter P

Trace and write the letters.
Start at the red dot (●).

P P P

p p p

Color the picture.

Fun Fact

Penguins are birds that can't fly, but they are excellent swimmers.

Trace the letters to finish the sentence. Start at the red dots (●).

P is for penguin.

The Letter Q

Trace and write the letters.
Start at the red dot (●).

Color the picture.

Trace the letters to finish the sentence. Start at the red dots (●).

Q is for quail.

The Letter R

Trace and write the letters.
Start at the red dot (●).

R R R

r r r

Color the picture.

Trace the letters to finish the sentence. Start at the red dots (●).

R is for robot.

The Letter S

Trace and write the letters.
Start at the red dot (●).

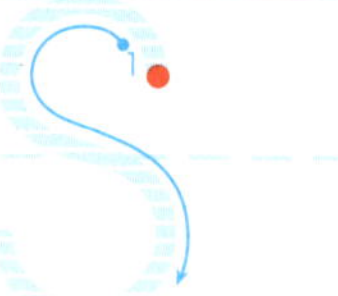

Color the picture.

Giggles

What is a snake's favorite subject in school?

Hisss-tory!

Trace the letters to finish the sentence. Start at the red dots (●).

S is for snake.

The Letter T

Trace and write the letters.
Start at the red dot (●).

Color the picture.

Trace the letters to finish the sentence. Start at the red dots (●).

T is for Tiger.

Lots of Letters

Say the name of each picture.
Underline the letters in each row that **begin** the name of the picture.

P D p b P

o O C Q o

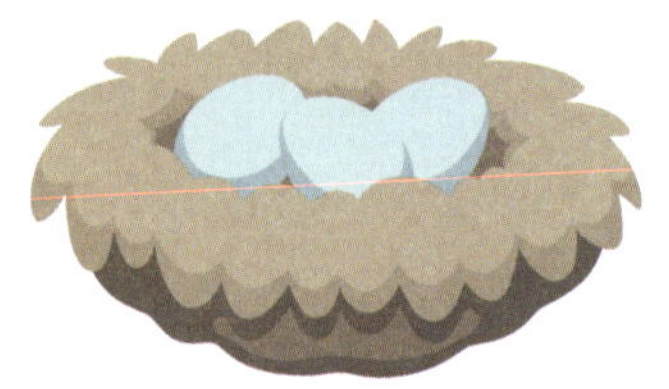

m N V n N

q Q o Q C

R n r P r

Matching Letters

Draw a line from each uppercase letter to the matching lowercase letter.

O	p
P	q
Q	o
R	t
S	r
T	s

The Letter U

Trace and write the letters.
Start at the red dot (●).

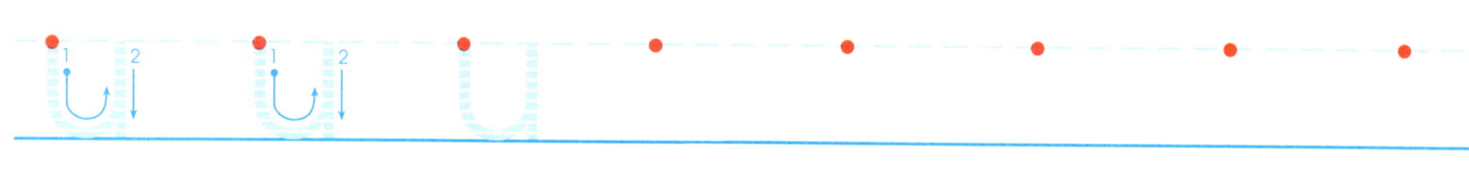

Color the picture.

Trace the letters to finish the sentence. Start at the red dots (●).

U is for umbrella.

The Letter V

Trace and write the letters.
Start at the red dot (●).

V V V

v v v

Color the picture.

Trace the letters to finish the sentence. Start at the red dots (●).

V is for violin.

The Letter W

Trace and write the letters.
Start at the red dot (•).

W W W

w w w

Color the picture.

Fun Fact

Both male and female walruses have tusks that keep growing all of their life.

Trace the letters to finish the sentence. Start at the red dots (•).

W is for walrus.

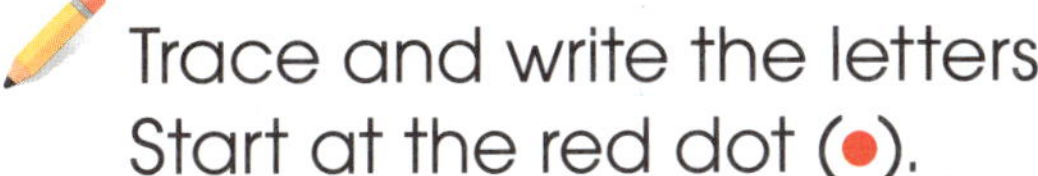

The Letter X

Trace and write the letters.
Start at the red dot (●).

X X X

x x x

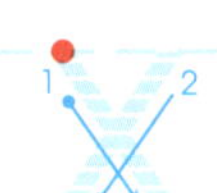

Color the picture.

Trace the letters to finish the sentence. Start at the red dots (●).

X is for x-ray fish.

The Letter Y

Trace and write the letters.
Start at the red dot (●).

Y Y Y

y y y

Color the picture.

Trace the letters to finish the sentence. Start at the red dots (●).

Y is for yak.

The Letter Z

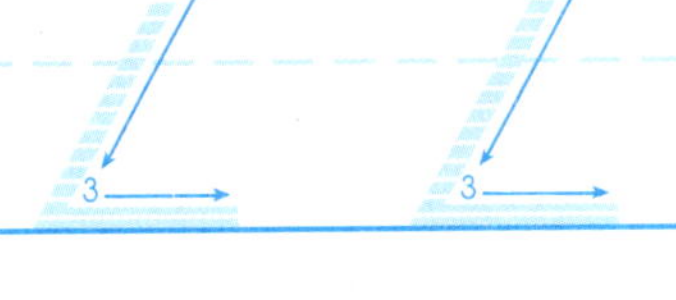

Trace and write the letters.
Start at the red dot (●).

Z Z Z

z z z

Color the picture.

Trace the letters to finish the sentence. Start at the red dots (●).

Z is for zebra.

Lots of Letters

Say the name of each picture.
Underline the letters in each row that **begin** the name of the picture.

U J u a U

S z s S r

W v V V N

t H T f T

Matching Letters

Draw a line from each uppercase letter to the matching lowercase letter.

U	w
V	v
W	x
X	u
Y	z
Z	y

What Letter Comes After?

C comes **after B**.
Write the letter that comes **after** each letter.
The first one is done for you.

A B C D E F G H I J K L M N O P Q R S T U V W X Y Z

B C

C

J

S

H

N

W

Y

What Letter Comes Between?

B comes **between A** and **C**.

Write the letter that comes **between** the letters.
The first one is done for you.

A B C D E F G H I J K L M N O P Q R S T U V W X Y Z

A B C   I _ K

P _ R   L _ N

T _ V   R _ T

X _ Z   D _ F

What Letter Comes Before?

A comes **before B**.
Write the letter that comes **before** each letter.
The first one is done for you.

A B C D E F G H I J K L M N O P Q R S T U V W X Y Z

A B

C

D

O

Y

R

G

M

Beginning Sounds

Circle the **beginning** sound for each picture.

c d

b r

n m

r u

k s

i l

v w

o c

What Letter Comes First?

Say the name of each picture.
Write **m** or **p** to **begin** each word.

____ig

____an

____ie

____om

Consonant Sounds

Say the name of each picture.
Draw a line from each picture to its **beginning** letter.

More Consonant Sounds

Say the name of each picture.
Draw a line from each picture to its **beginning** letter.

s

w

h

z

b

More Consonant Sounds

Say the name of each picture.
Draw a line from each picture to its **beginning** letter.

m

Beginning Letter Sounds

Draw a line from each word to the matching picture.

cat

bat

hat

Write the missing letter to make each word.

__at

__at

__at

Ending Sounds

Circle the **ending** sound for each picture.

s t

y p

g r

m f

t x

b d

More Ending Sounds

Circle the **ending** sound for each picture.

v n

s r

g m

k h

k t

d b

What Letter Goes at the End?

Say the name of each picture.
Write **m** or **n** to **end** each word.

Giggles
Why did the sun go to school?
To get brighter!

su___

gu___

moo___

fa___

What Letter Goes at the End?

Say the name of each picture.
Write **d** or **t** to **end** each word.

goa___

bir___

da___

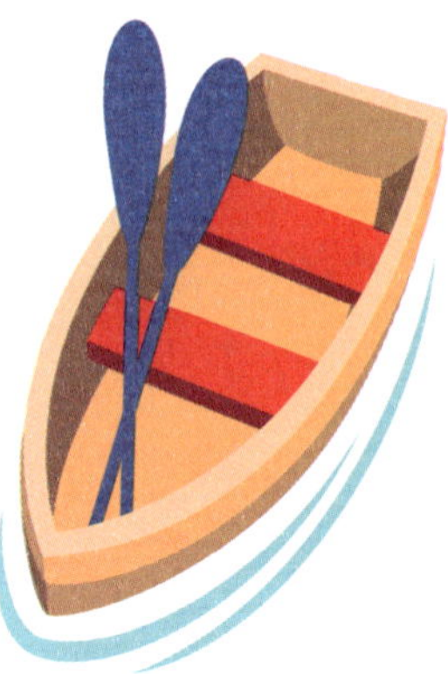

boa___

Short a Words

Say the names of the pictures.
Write the letters to make **short a** words.
The first one is done for you.

bat **cat** **fan** **pan**

Short e Words

short e sound as in **nest**

Say the names of the pictures.
Write the letters to make **short e** words.

bed **net** **pen** **web**

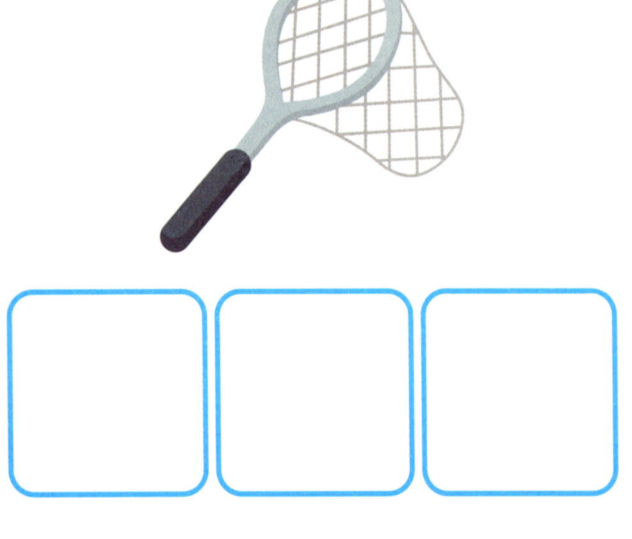

Fun Fact
A spider is not an insect. Spiders have 8 legs. Insects have 6.

Short i Words

short i sound as in **igloo**

Say the names of the pictures.
Write the letters to make **short i** words.

pig **pin** **fin** **six**

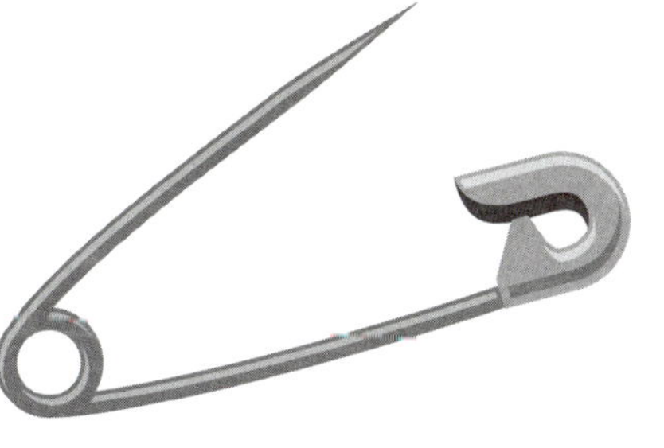

Short o Words

short o sound
as in **octopus**

Giggles

How do you make an octopus laugh?

With ten-tickles!

Say the names of the pictures.
Write the letters to make **short o** words.

pot **fox** **mop** **box**

Short u Words

short u sound
as in **umbrella**

Say the names of the pictures.
Write the letters to make **short u** words.

bus **cup** **sun** **bug**

Short Vowel Sounds

Say the name of each picture.
Circle the picture that has each **short vowel** sound.

Short a

Short e

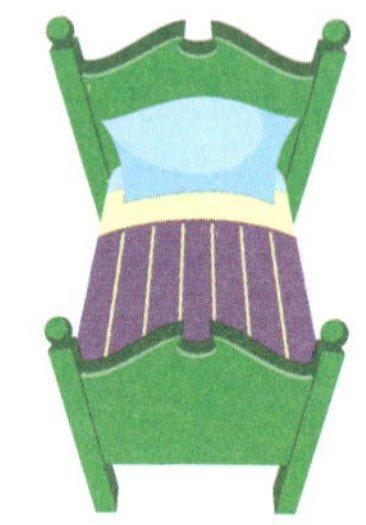

Short i

Short o

Short u

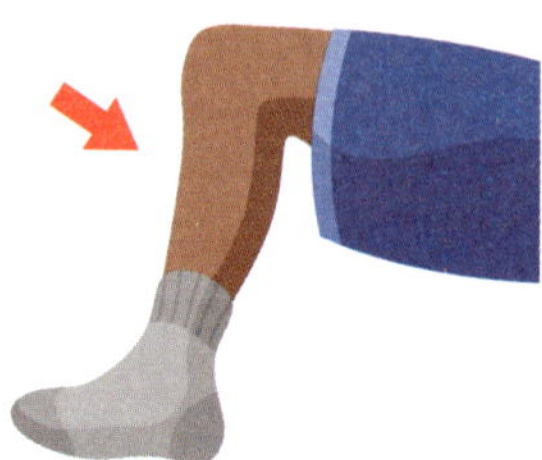

More Short Vowel Sounds

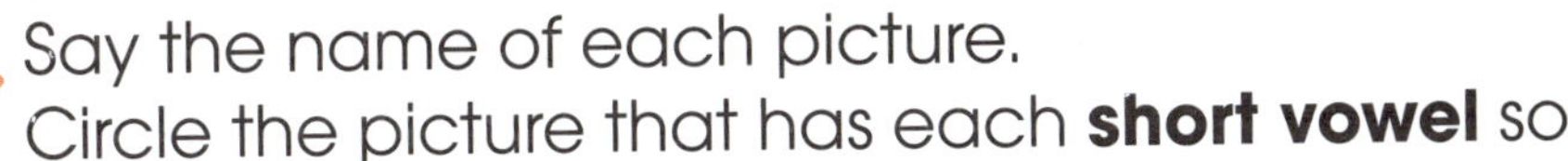

Say the name of each picture.
Circle the picture that has each **short vowel** sound.

Short a

Short e

Short i

Short o

Short u

Greater Than

Greater means **more than**.

5 **is greater than 4.**

Count the number of birds on each branch.
Write the number in the box.
Circle the group that has **more** birds.

Less Than

Which group has fewer objects?
Match the objects one-to-one.
Circle the number that is **less**.
The first one is done for you.

Try This!

Learn to Count—Snack Time Fun
Use 5 small paper plates. Write a number, 1 to 5, on each plate. Have kids count snacks onto each plate to match the number. A yummy lesson!

2

4

5

8

7

4

Adding With 5-Frames

How many are there **in all**?
Write the number.
The first one is done for you.

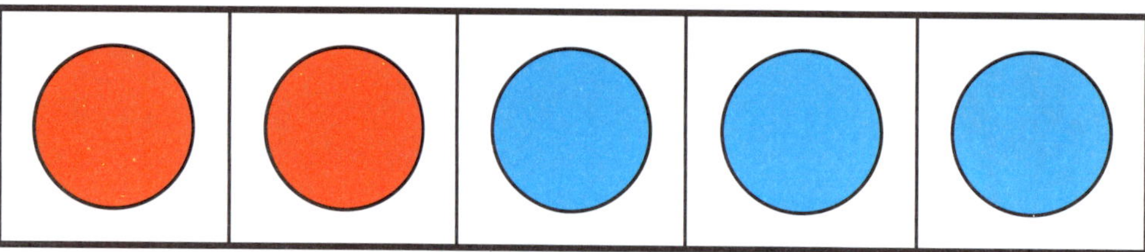

2 + 3 = 5

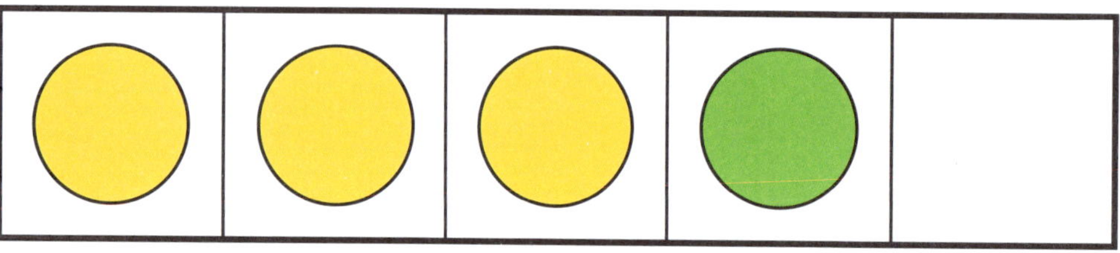

3 + 1 = ____

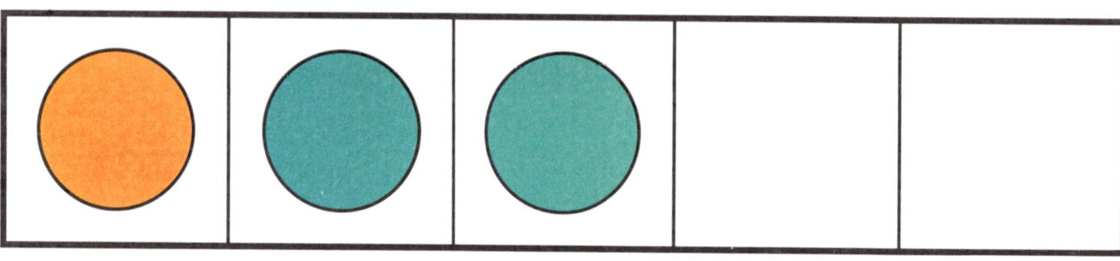

1 + 2 = ____

More Adding With 5-Frames

How many are there **altogether**?
Write the number.

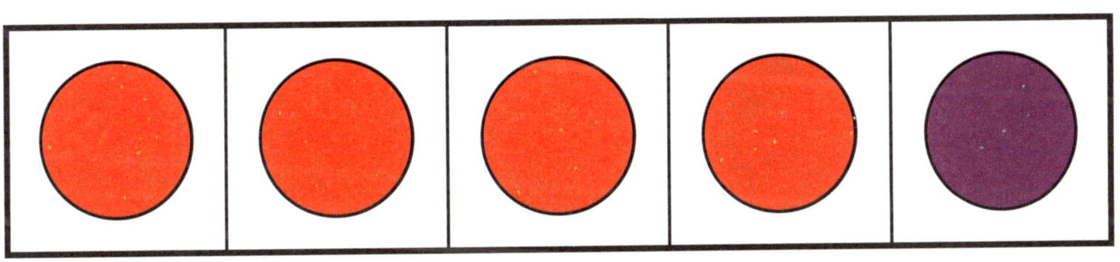

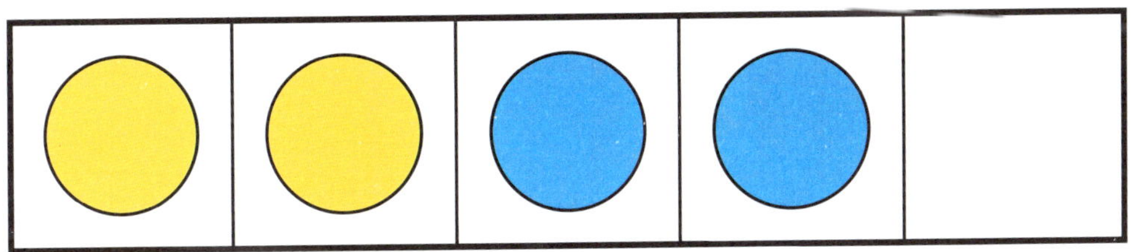

2 + 2 =

Adding With 10-Frames

How many are there **in all**?
Write the number.

Parent Tip
If this is easy for your child, repeat these activities with objects such as pennies with answers up to 10.

6 + 3 = ____

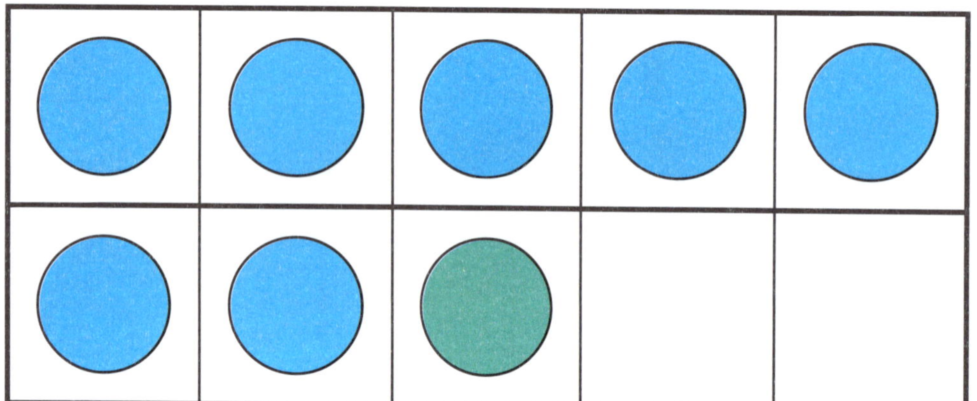

7 + 1 = ____

More Adding With 10-Frames

How many are there **altogether**?
Write the number.

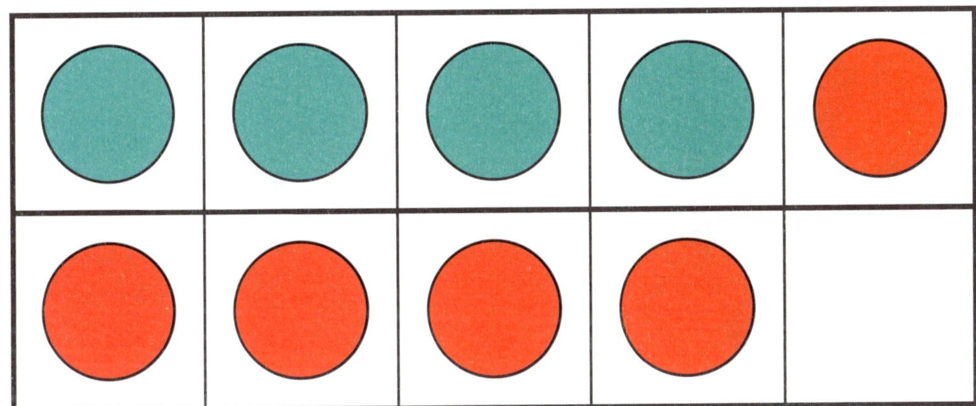

4 + 5 = ____

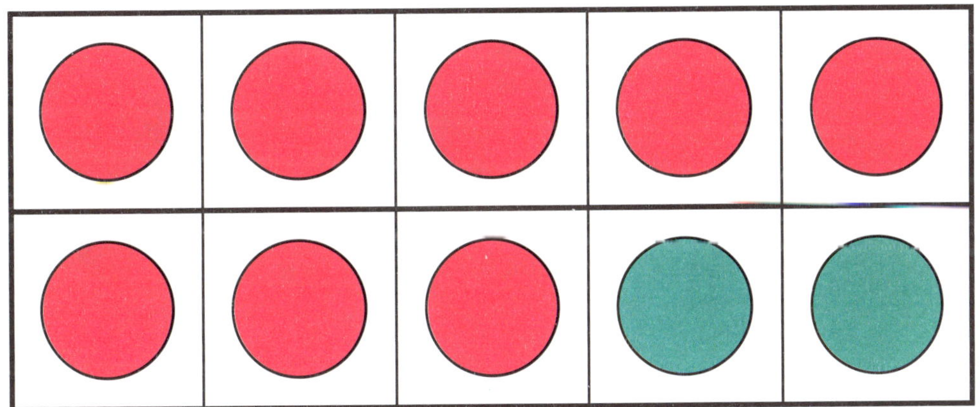

8 + 2 = ____

Addition

How many are there **in all**?
Write the number.

2 + 2 = ____

3 + 2 = ____

1 + 2 = ____

4 + 2 = ____

More Addition

How many are there **altogether**?
Write the number.

1 + 4 = ____

5 + 2 = ____

3 + 3 = ____

7 + 1 = ____

Wordsearch for a Summer Day

Find and circle the words in the list below. Words are only going across.

CAN	NOT	BIG	WHERE
SEE	ONE	COME	JUMP

C	O	M	E	X	L	T	K	G	W
N	V	O	Q	E	Q	B	I	G	M
J	N	I	D	W	H	E	R	E	D
D	O	Y	V	S	N	J	E	N	Y
I	M	W	Y	I	W	K	X	F	H
J	U	M	P	U	J	I	C	A	N
W	V	J	C	N	H	N	G	H	V
S	Q	O	N	E	Z	L	S	E	E
E	L	X	E	V	W	Q	A	M	T
R	C	J	N	O	T	Z	B	D	G